THE EASTER STORY
CARINE MACKENZIE

ILLUSTRATED BY
NATASCIA UGLIANO

A gift given with love to:

....

....

From:

....

....

Contents

1. Tell Me the Story of Easter

Easter is a celebration. In some parts of the world it takes place at Spring time when new plants are beginning to grow and baby animals are being born. But in other parts of the world Spring time happens at other times of the year.

Thankfully the story of Easter is something that we can celebrate and read about at any time of the year. It can be Spring, but this is also a story for Summer, Autumn or Winter. The story is true, it's real and it can change your life!

2. One Moment in Time

The Easter Story is the most amazing event in history. In one moment of time, the Lord Jesus Christ took the punishment for the sins of all his followers, when he died on the cross. This was not a

tragic accident. It was God's plan for the salvation of his people. Jesus gave his life willingly as a sacrifice for sin.

The Easter Story is not just about the death of Jesus, but also about his resurrection. God raised him from death on the third day. He appeared to many people and then he ascended into heaven and is alive for evermore – King of kings and Lord of lords. Let's look at some of the details of this story of God's love for sinners.

3. Journey to Jerusalem

Jesus and the disciples went to Bethany, a town near Jerusalem, to have a meal. Mary came over to Jesus and poured some very expensive ointment from an alabaster flask all over Jesus' feet. 'What a waste!' Judas Iscariot exclaimed. 'That ointment could have been sold and the money given to the poor.'

'Don't trouble her,' said Jesus. 'She has anointed me in preparation for my burial. I will not always be with you.'

Jesus knew he would soon die.

Jesus and his disciples made the journey to the city of Jerusalem. Jesus knew that he would have to face suffering and death. However, he knew it was his Father's will and he was obedient. When they came near the Mount of Olives, Jesus called two of his disciples over to him.

'Go to that village,' he said. 'You will find a young colt tethered. It has never been ridden before. Untie it and bring it to me. If anyone asks you what you are doing, tell them that the Lord needs it.'

The disciples found the colt exactly as Jesus had described. The owners asked them what they were doing, but were agreeable when they were told, 'The Lord needs it.'

They brought the colt to Jesus, threw their cloaks on it and helped Jesus up on its back. As Jesus rode along the road, some people took their cloaks or cut down leafy branches and put them on the road.

4. Greedy Men and Singing Children

As they left the Mount of Olives, the disciples began to shout and sing praises to God. The crowd of people who were following joined in too, 'Hosanna! Blessed is the King who comes in the name of the Lord. Peace in heaven and glory in the highest!'

Jesus rode into Jerusalem with shouts of triumph and praise ringing in his ears – like a victorious king. In the temple, Jesus chased away the

greedy men who used God's house as a
trading place. He overturned the tables
of the money-changers and the seats of the
pigeon-sellers.

Some blind and lame people came to Jesus in the temple and he
healed them. Jesus was pleased to hear the children singing praises and
cheering. But this made some of the temple leaders very annoyed. They
were so angry, in fact, that they plotted to kill Jesus.

5. Thirty Pieces of Silver

When Judas Iscariot learned that the chief priests wanted to get rid of Jesus, he offered to help them catch him. They agreed to give Judas thirty pieces of silver, if he would betray Jesus.

On the day of the Passover Feast, Jesus sent two of his disciples into the city to get the meal ready.

'You will see a man carrying a jar of water,' Jesus

told them. 'Follow him. At the house he enters, tell

the man in charge that your master has sent you to see the room, where

we will eat the Passover.'

The man showed them to a large upstairs room, furnished and ready.

They prepared the supper.

In the evening, Jesus and the other disciples joined them for the Passover

Feast of roast lamb, bread and wine.

6. The Servant King

uring supper, Jesus got up, tied a towel round his waist and filled a basin with water. He then began to wash the disciples' feet and dry them with the towel. This was a task that the lowliest servant in the household would usually do. Peter objected, 'You should not be washing my feet.'

'If I do not wash you,' Jesus answered, 'you will have no part with me.'

'Oh!' declared Peter, 'not just my feet then but my hands and my head too.'

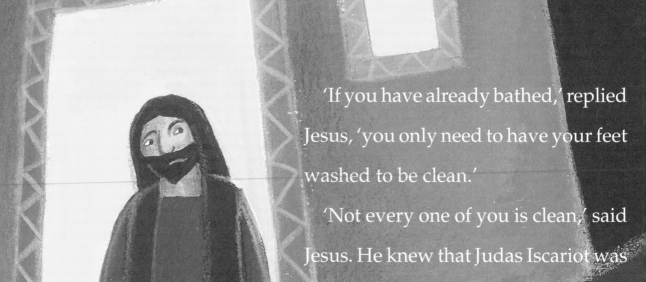

'If you have already bathed,' replied Jesus, 'you only need to have your feet washed to be clean.'

'Not every one of you is clean,' said Jesus. He knew that Judas Iscariot was going to betray him.

Jesus knew what was in Judas' mind. During the supper he said, 'One of you shall betray me.'

The disciples were naturally upset. One by one they asked, 'Is it I?' Then John said, 'Tell us who it is.'

'It is the man,' Jesus replied, 'to whom I shall give this piece of bread.'

He took the bread, dipped it into the dish and handed it to Judas Iscariot.

Immediately Judas left the room and went out into the dark night.

7. Love One Another

The Passover Meal took on a new meaning that night. Jesus was preparing his followers for his death. As he broke the bread and handed it round, he said, 'This is my body which is given for you.' Then he passed round a cup of wine and said, 'This is my blood. When you eat the bread and drink the wine, remember me.'

We call this the Lord's Supper. Followers of Jesus all over the world remember him in this way.

'I am giving you a new commandment,' Jesus said. 'You should love one another just as I have loved you. People will know that you are my disciples if you love one another.'

Jesus told them plainly that he was going away, but that he would come back again. He would ask God the Father to send the Holy Spirit to be their helper.

'Do not be troubled or afraid,' said Jesus. 'I give my peace to you.'

Then they sang a hymn and went out to the Mount of Olives.

'You will all be ashamed of me tonight,' Jesus told them.

Peter answered, 'Lord, I will never be ashamed of you, even if everyone else is.'

'I am telling you, Peter,' said Jesus, 'before the cock crows twice in the morning, you will deny three times that you know me.'

'I will never deny you!' exclaimed Peter, 'even if I have to die with you.'

8. Sleeping in the Garden

Peter seemed very brave and sure of himself but Jesus knew him better.

Jesus went to the Garden of Gethsemane to pray. He asked Peter, James and John to sit nearby while he prayed to his Father in heaven. Jesus knew what great suffering he was facing. He was very sad.

After he prayed, Jesus came back to Peter and the other two disciples and found them all sleeping. He said to Peter, 'Could you not watch with me for one hour?'

Jesus went to pray again. When he came back the second time he found them all asleep again.

After they had fallen asleep a third time, Jesus said, 'You can sleep on now.'

9. Swords in the Garden

Judas Iscariot knew that the Garden of Gethsemane was a favourite place for Jesus to spend time praying.

He came to the garden with a large mob of men armed with swords and clubs, sent from the chief priests and scribes and elders.

Jesus knew what was going to happen. He came towards the crowd.

'Who are you looking for?' he asked.

'Jesus of Nazareth,' they replied.

'I am he,' said Jesus simply.

The mob were amazed by Jesus' straight reply. Then Judas confirmed Jesus' identity by greeting him with a treacherous kiss.

The men grabbed Jesus to take him away. Peter struck one of the men with a sword and cut off his ear. Jesus told Peter to put his sword away.

Jesus then healed the man's ear immediately.

The soldiers tied Jesus up and led him away. The disciples left him and fled. How things had changed since Jesus had ridden triumphantly into Jerusalem a few days before.

10. At the High Priest's Palace

The wicked men took Jesus to the palace of Caiaphas the high priest. There he endured a mockery of a trial. Many witnesses were brought to speak against him. They told lies. Their statements did not agree.

'Tell us,' demanded the high priest, 'whether you are Christ, the Son of God.'

Jesus answered, 'You have said it.'

The high priest was shocked. 'He has spoken blasphemy. We do not need any more witnesses.' They spat in his face and slapped him, mocking and jeering him.

Peter and another disciple had followed Jesus to the high priest's palace. A fire was burning in the middle of the courtyard. Peter sat down with the servants warming themselves in the chill of the early morning.

A young girl, who worked as a doorkeeper at the palace, recognised Peter. 'Were you not one of those who went about with Jesus of Nazareth?'

'Woman, I do not know him,' denied Peter.

Then Peter went to the porch, just as the cock was first crowing. Another girl said, 'This fellow was with Jesus of Nazareth too.'

Again Peter denied it. 'I do not know the man.'

11. Before the Cock Crows

An hour later someone else said confidently, 'I am sure you were with Jesus for you speak like a Galilean too.'

'I do not know who you are talking about!' Peter replied in a panic.

Immediately, the cock crew for the second time. Jesus turned and looked at Peter. Peter remembered what Jesus had said, 'Before the cock crows twice you will deny me three times.'

Peter had been so sure that he would stand up for Jesus. But he failed. He went outside and wept bitterly.

As soon as it was morning, Jesus was tied up again and taken to Pilate the governor of the land.

'Are you the King of the Jews?' asked Pilate.

'You have said so,' replied Jesus.

Pilate went out to the Jewish throng. 'I do not find him guilty of any crime.'

The people would not accept this judgement.

'He is a troublemaker. He stirs up the people by his teaching and preaching throughout the land.'

12. Crucify Him!

Pilate tried to pass the responsibility on to King Herod who was in Jerusalem at that time. Herod was pleased to meet this man, Jesus whom he had heard so much about. Perhaps he would see some miracle, he thought. He questioned him again and again, but Jesus remained silent. Herod and his soldiers made fun of Jesus and sent him back to Pilate.

Pilate tried another tactic.

'There is a custom that a prisoner is released at this time of the Passover Feast. Will you allow me to release Jesus the King of the Jews?'

'No!' the crowd shouted. 'Not this man. Release Barabbas!'

Barabbas was a murderer and robber, now in prison for his crimes.

'What will I do to Jesus?' asked Pilate.

'Let him be crucified!' they all said.

Pilate tried again, 'I will punish him and let him go.'

The cry became stronger, 'Crucify him! Crucify him! Release Barabbas!'

13. Mocking the Messiah

Eventually, Pilate gave in to their demands. He took some water and washed his hands. 'I am innocent of killing this good man,' he said.

He foolishly thought that washing his hands would cleanse the guilt of his part in handing over Jesus to the soldiers.

The soldiers took Jesus, stripped off his clothes and put on him a royal robe. They made a crown of thorns and pushed it on his head. They put a reed in his hand like a sceptre. Then they pretended to bow down to him, making fun of him.

Still, Pilate insisted weakly, 'I find no fault in him. Take him away yourselves and crucify him.'

'He must die, because he says he is the Son of God,' they claimed. When Pilate heard that, he was even more afraid.

Jesus was led away to be crucified.

14. Father Forgive Them

rucifixion was a cruel death – being nailed to a wooden cross. Jesus was forced to carry this big, wooden cross on his back at first but then they allowed him to get help from a man called Simon. Crowds of people followed him. Many women were crying loudly.

When they reached a place called Calvary they nailed Jesus' hands and feet to the cross and lifted it up. Even then Jesus prayed to God, 'Father, forgive them, for they do not realise what they are doing.' What love he showed.

The soldiers took Jesus' garment and cut it up into four parts. Each of them took a piece. His coat was made of one complete piece. 'Let's cast lots,' one of them said, 'and the winner can take it all.' Even that small detail had been foretold in the book of Psalms hundreds of years before.

15. Remember Me!

Jesus' mother, Mary, and some other women were standing near the cross. Even during his pain Jesus noticed his mother. 'Woman, behold your son,' he said. To his beloved disciple John, he said, 'Behold your mother.' From then on John took Mary to his own home to look after her.

Two thieves were crucified along with Jesus. One complained to Jesus, 'If you are the Christ, why can't you save yourself and us?'

'How can you speak like that?' the other thief said. 'We deserve all this punishment, but this man has done nothing wrong.' He knew Jesus was indeed the Son of God. Then he turned to him and said, 'Remember me when you come into your kingdom.'

Jesus gave him far more. 'Today you will be with me in Paradise,' he promised.

In the final moments of his life, this man, who had done great wrong, asked Jesus for mercy. Jesus showed him love by forgiving his sin.

16. It is Finished!

It was twelve noon and there was darkness over the land until three o'clock. Jesus reached the depths of his suffering.

He called out to God, 'My God, my God, why have you left me?' He was completely alone.

When he called out, 'I am thirsty!' he was given a sponge soaked in vinegar. After Jesus had drunk some vinegar, he called out, 'It is finished!' and then with a loud voice, 'Father, into your hands I commend my spirit.'

He then bowed his head and gave up his spirit.

Jesus' death fulfilled a wonderful plan of salvation for his people. All sin deserves to be punished. By suffering and dying for the sin of those who trust in him, Jesus took the full punishment for all their sins. He had power to lay down his life and power to take it again. Jesus obeyed God his Father, and gave up his life willingly to save lost sinners.

At the moment of Jesus' death the big curtain in the temple was torn in two from top to bottom, the earth trembled, the rocks were split open. Some tombs were also opened and the bodies of some godly people were raised to life.

One of the soldiers keeping watch was very afraid. 'Truly, this was the Son of God,' he said.

17. The Rich Man's Tomb

Before the soldiers took the bodies of Jesus and the thieves down from the crosses, they broke the legs of the thieves to make sure that they were dead. But Jesus was already dead so they did not break his legs. A soldier thrust a spear into Jesus' side. Out poured blood and water.

A rich man called Joseph went to Pilate and asked to bury Jesus in his own tomb. His request was granted, so Joseph, helped by Nicodemus, took Jesus' body from the cross and wrapped it in linen cloths with spices of myrrh and aloes. They carefully laid Jesus' body in the tomb, which was a cave cut out of the rock. They rolled a big stone over the mouth of the cave.

The chief priests and religious leaders reminded Pilate that Jesus had said he would rise from the dead on the third day.

'Give orders that the tomb is made very secure until the third day,' they said, 'just in case his disciples come and steal his body and say he is risen.'

'Go,' said Pilate, 'and make it as secure as you can.'

So the stone was specially sealed and a guard set to keep watch.

Very early in the morning, on the first day of the week, Mary Magdalene and two other ladies came to where Jesus had been buried. They wanted to anoint Jesus' body with spices. They were concerned about the big stone at the door of the tomb. Who would roll it away they wondered.

When they reached the tomb, however, the stone had already been rolled away and an angel was sitting on it.

18. He is Risen!

Mary Magdalene ran to tell Peter and John what had happened. The others looked inside the tomb and found two angels. 'Do not be afraid,' one said. 'I know you are looking for Jesus. He is not here. He has risen from the dead.'

Peter and John came running when they heard the news. They looked into the tomb and saw the linen grave clothes lying where Jesus had been. They went back home wondering about all the things that had happened.

Mary Magdalene came back to the garden. She was weeping with sorrow because she thought Jesus' body had been stolen. She spoke to a man she thought was the gardener. The man spoke her name, 'Mary!'

She immediately realised that he was the risen Lord Jesus.

'Master!' she cried out.

Mary ran with the good news to the disciples.

19. Who is the Stranger?

Cleopas and his friend were walking to Emmaus, talking about all that had happened in Jerusalem during the past few days.

Jesus himself came along beside them but they thought he was a stranger.

'What are you speaking about?' asked Jesus.

'Don't you know what's been happening in Jerusalem?' they asked.

'What things?' replied Jesus.

'The things that happened to Jesus,' they said.

'He was condemned to death. We had hoped he would be the Saviour of our people. Three days have passed since his death. Some women found his tomb empty. Angels said he was alive. Some others went to the tomb, but did not see Jesus.'

Jesus gently rebuked them. 'Do you not know the Messiah had to suffer all these things before he entered glory?' Jesus then explained to them all the Old Testament Scriptures about himself.

When they reached Emmaus they persuaded the stranger to come into the house for some food, for it was late. When they sat down for supper, Jesus took the bread, blessed it and handed them a piece. Only then did they recognise him. Immediately he vanished from their sight.

20. Doubting Thomas

Hurrying back to Jerusalem they shared the good news with the eleven disciples and other followers. 'The Lord is risen,' they said.

One evening, Jesus entered the room where the disciples were meeting, even though the doors were locked. 'Peace be to you,' he said. He showed them his hands and side which had been pierced on the cross. Thomas was not there at that time. When he heard, he could not believe it.

'Unless I see the marks in his hands and put my
hand in his side, I will never believe.'

Eight days later, when Jesus came again, he
said to Thomas, 'See my hands. Put your hand
into my side. Do not doubt, but believe.'

'My Lord and my God!' declared Thomas.

'Have you believed because you have seen me?' asked
Jesus. 'Blessed are those who have not seen and yet
have believed.'

21. Breakfast on the Beach

Some time later seven of the disciples went fishing on the Sea of Galilee. They fished all night, but caught nothing. As they came back to the beach they noticed a man standing there watching them.

'Have you any food?' he asked. 'No,' they replied.

'Put your net down again on the right side of the boat,' he said. When they did so, they caught a huge number of fish. John then recognised that the man was Jesus. 'It is the Lord,' he said.

Peter jumped into the sea to reach the shore ahead of the boat. On the shore Jesus had a fire lit with fish already cooking and bread. Jesus invited them to bring some of the fish they had caught too. They had a lovely breakfast together.

The Lord Jesus was seen and recognised by many people during the forty days that he lived on earth after his resurrection. He instructed his followers to go out into the world and preach the gospel.

He led them out of the city of Jerusalem to the Mount of Olives. 'I will send the Holy Spirit to help you and you will be my witnesses right to the furthest corner of the earth.'

He lifted up his hands and blessed them. His body ascended up to heaven and soon a cloud hid him from sight. Two men in white clothes stood there and spoke to the disciples, 'Why are you staring up to heaven? Just as you have seen Jesus taken up to heaven, he will return to earth one day.'

The disciples worshipped God and went, joyfully, back to Jerusalem to start preaching the Good News about Jesus.

Followers of Jesus are still telling the wonderful story of Easter – the Good News that Jesus died for our sins, rose again from the dead and ascended to heaven, a Prince and a Saviour.

For God so loved the World that he gave his only Son - Jesus!

If we trust in him, we have the sure hope of eternal life with him in heaven.

Christian Focus Publications publishes books for adults and children under its four main imprints: Christian Focus, Christian Heritage, CF4K and Mentor. Our books reflect that God's Word is reliable and Jesus is the way to know him, and live for ever with him.

Our children's publication list includes a Sunday school curriculum that covers pre-school to early teens; puzzle and activity books. We also publish personal and family devotional titles, biographies and inspirational stories that children will love.

If you are looking for quality Bible teaching for children then we have an excellent range of Bible story and age specific theological books. From pre-school to teenage fiction, we have it covered!

Find us at our web page: www.christianfocus.com

10 9 8 7 6 5 4 3 2 1

© Copyright 2015 Carine Mackenzie

ISBN: 978-1-78191-566-0

Published by Christian Focus Publications,
Geanies House, Fearn, Tain, Ross-shire,
IV20 1TW, Scotland, U.K.

Cover design: Daniel van Straaten

Illustrations by Natascia Ugliano

Printed by Gutenberg in Malta

Scripture quotations are the author's own paraphrase.